Kingdom Files:

Who Was Mary, Mother of Jesus?

Kingdom Files:

Who Was Mary, Mother of Jesus?

Matt Koceich

BARBOUR BOOKS
An Imprint of Barbour Publishing, Inc.

Print ISBN 978-1-68322-631-4

eBook Editions:
Adobe Digital Edition (.epub) 978-1-68322-899-8
Kindle and MobiPocket Edition (.prc) 978-1-68322-905-6

Cover design by C. B. Canga
Interior illustration by Patricia Yuste

Published by Barbour Books, an imprint of Barbour Publishing, Inc., 1810 Barbour Drive, Uhrichsville, Ohio 44683, www.barbourbooks.com

Our mission is to inspire the world with the life-changing message of the Bible.

Member of the
Evangelical Christian
Publishers Association

Printed in the United States of America.

06136 0718 CM

Dear Reading Detective,

Welcome to Kingdom Files! You're now a very important part of the Kingdom Files investigation—a series of really cool biographies all found in the Bible. Each case you investigate focuses on an important Bible character and is separated into three sections to make your time fun and interesting. First, you'll find the **Fact File**, which contains key information about a specific Bible character whom God called to do big things for His kingdom. Next, you'll read through an **Action File** that lays out Bible events showing the character in action. And finally, the **Power File** is where you'll find valuable information and memory verses to help you see how God is working in your life too. Along the way, **Clue Boxes** will offer applications to help you keep track of your thoughts as you make your way through the files. You can also use these sections to record questions you might have along Mary's journey. Write down any questions, and then ask your parents to get them involved in your quest.

Before you begin, know this: not only did God have plans for the Bible characters you'll read about in the Kingdom Files, but Jeremiah 29:11 says that God has big plans for you too! I pray that *Kingdom Files: Who Was Mary, Mother of Jesus?* helps you get a bigger picture of God, and that you will see just how much He loves you!

Blessings,

M.K.

Name: **MARY**

Occupation: **mother of Jesus**

From: **Nazareth**

Years Active: **around 5 BC–AD 33**

Kingdom Work: **raised Jesus
and protected Him from Herod;
followed Jesus' teachings;
prayed for God's will to be done**

Key Stats:

+ Gave birth to
Jesus

+ Obeyed His
teachings

+ Prayed with
other believers
for the Holy
Spirit

Mini Timeline:

5 BC
Gives
birth
to Jesus

2 BC
Flees to
Egypt

AD 12
Finds
Jesus
in temple

AD 27
Wedding
at Cana

AD 31
Witnesses
Jesus'
crucifixion

1

Great News!

Mary played a very special part in God's kingdom work. She was the young woman God chose to be the mother of Jesus! Her world was about to be turned upside down in a miraculous way.

A long time before Mary became pregnant, the prophet Isaiah talked about this special moment in history. This moment was special because God had chosen to send His only Son, Jesus, to be born of a virgin. It was so special because He was sending His only Son to take on flesh and become the Savior of the world. The prophet said that Mary would give birth to a son and name him Immanuel, which means "God with us" (Isaiah 7:14; Matthew 1:23).

An angel named Gabriel visited Mary in her
hometown of Nazareth in Galilee. This small

town was twelve miles south of the Sea of Galilee, situated on a high hill far away from the main roads. Nazareth held to strong Jewish traditions. It had a tiny population of less than five hundred people. The Nazarenes were farmers who raised livestock and planted orchards. The people spoke a language called Aramaic.

Gabriel said, "Greetings, you who are highly favored! The Lord is with you" (Luke 1:28). Mary was young (most likely not older than fifteen), and she was overwhelmed at the angel's words. Mary didn't understand the angel's message. Out of all the girls in the world at that time, God chose her for a very unique role. The angel went on to comfort Mary and remind her that she didn't need to be afraid. The angel said this about Jesus: "He will be great and will be called the Son of the Most High.... His kingdom will never end" (Luke 1:32–33).

Even though Mary didn't understand everything that was happening, she told the angel that she was the Lord's servant. She said, "May your word to me be fulfilled" (Luke 1:38). This gives us a good understanding of her relationship with God and her strong faith. Mary was pledged to wed a man named Joseph. Before they were actually married, a miracle happened and Mary was "found to be pregnant through the Holy Spirit" (Matthew 1:18).

This was a very stressful time for Mary, because in the culture of Mary's day, people wouldn't have understood what really happened. They would have judged her. Can you imagine all the stares and weird looks Mary must have received because of her pregnancy? And then when people would ask her to explain, Mary would begin her story with an angel appearing to her. That would surely have made people roll their eyes. Mary must have felt alone and afraid.

Joseph didn't want to bring any disgrace to Mary, so "he had in mind to divorce her quietly" (Matthew 1:19). That's when an angel appeared to

Joseph in a dream and told him not to be afraid to take Mary as his wife. The angel went on to explain that something very miraculous had happened

and that the baby inside Mary's belly was conceived from the Holy Spirit (Matthew 1:20). The angel also told Joseph that they were to name the baby Jesus because He was going to save people from their sins! After this message from the angel, Joseph and Mary became husband and wife.

At this time, Mary had a family member named Elizabeth who lived far away in a land called Judea. Mary left Nazareth and traveled the long distance to Judea after receiving news from the angel about her pregnancy. This escape to the hills would at least help Mary endure the first few months of her pregnancy away from curious villagers who wouldn't understand or believe her story.

When Mary arrived at her relative's house, she received

some really amazing news. Elizabeth was also pregnant! Her child was John the Baptist, who would be the one to share the good news of Jesus, the Messiah.

When Mary arrived at the door and greeted Elizabeth, the baby in Elizabeth's womb leaped for joy! Elizabeth immediately understood what had happened to Mary. She said to her, "Blessed are you among women, and blessed is the child you will bear!" (Luke 1:42). This helped Mary to know even more that she really was being used by God in a special way. Remember that Mary was only a young teenager. Her faith and obedience to God are what helped her each step of the way along the path God had for her.

Mary responded to Elizabeth by singing a song:

My soul glorifies the Lord
and my spirit rejoices in God my Savior,
for he has been mindful
of the humble state of his servant.
From now on all generations will call me blessed,
for the Mighty One has done great things for me—
holy is his name.
His mercy extends to those who fear him,
from generation to generation.
He has performed mighty deeds with his arm;
he has scattered those who are proud in their
inmost thoughts.

He has brought down rulers from their thrones

but has lifted up the humble.

He has filled the hungry with good things

but has sent the rich away empty.

He has helped his servant Israel, remembering

to be merciful

to Abraham and his descendants forever,

just as he promised our ancestors. (Luke 1:46–55)

This was a beautiful expression of Mary's faith.

Even though she was young, her heart was filled with joy because of who God is. Another neat thing about Mary's song is that she was quoting the Psalms. It's encouraging to see a girl so young who was very much connected to the Word of God. The Bible also shows that Jesus came from the line of King David, who wrote many of the psalms that Mary referred to in her song.

David sang, "Praise the LORD, my soul; all my inmost being, praise his holy name" (Psalm 103:1). Mary sang the same, also saying that her soul brings God glory (Luke 1:46) and that

CLUES

Mary's song reminds us to always praise God, for He is worthy. God gives us grace. He fills our hearts and keeps all His promises.

God's name is holy (v. 49). And if you read Psalm 8, you will find David singing these words: "What is mankind that you are mindful of them?" (v. 4). In

Psalm 138, David again reflected on this same topic: "Though the LORD is exalted, he looks kindly on the lowly" (v. 6).

Mary stayed with Elizabeth for three months and then returned home to Nazareth.

O Holy Night

Over two thousand years ago, when Mary was about to give birth to baby Jesus, an order was given saying that a census should be taken. A census is when the government counts the number of people living in certain areas. At this time in history, the Roman Empire was in control of all the lands that were around in the times of Jesus. The emperor was a man named Caesar Augustus. He had been in charge for twenty-five years, and plans for celebrations were under way.

The order required everyone travel to their hometowns to register and pay taxes. Joseph was from Bethlehem, so he took Mary with him and left Nazareth.

The journey for Mary and Joseph would have

been about eighty miles total. They most likely

traveled to Jerusalem first and then made their

way on to Bethlehem. Mary and Joseph probably

made the trek with a group of people who were also

going to different towns to register for the census.

The trip wasn't easy for Mary since she was several

months into her pregnancy (Luke 2:4–5). Also,

their route would have taken them through a land

called Samaria. The Samaritans weren't friends with the Jewish people, so this would have added stress to Mary's already overwhelmed heart. The whole journey likely took them more than a week to complete, and Mary probably made the trip riding on the back of a donkey.

Joseph and Mary arrived in Bethlehem and tried to find room at an inn. Mary must have been very tired, but she soon heard that there was no

space available for them. Many people were traveling because of the census, and all the places to stay were already occupied. And because Joseph and Mary were poor, no accommodations were made for them. Can you imagine? Mary was so close to having baby Jesus, but there was nowhere for her and Joseph to go. At some point, after hearing there wasn't a room for them, Mary and Joseph were given permission to stay in a stable. This might have been a cave close to the inn where the other guests stayed.

A stable is where cattle were kept. Even though we don't know for sure what Mary was thinking, we can be certain that she was not very comfortable. Worn out from the pregnancy and the long, hard trip, Mary had to wonder where God was in all this. She knew that her baby was special and that the Holy Spirit was with her,

CLUES

Everything about this holy night seemed the opposite of how Jesus, the King of all kings, should have entered the world. But Mary chose to believe God was on her side and hadn't forgotten about her and the baby.

but her emotions in the moment had to be overwhelming. Still, Mary trusted God. She knew that God was in charge and that He wouldn't let her down.

As soon as Jesus was born, Mary wrapped Jesus in cloths and put Him down to sleep in a manger. The manger was a trough, likely carved

from stone, from which the animals ate their food.

While Mary and Joseph were huddled with the dirty animals in the stable, caring for baby Jesus, another group of people were taking care of important things. Some shepherds were living out in the nearby fields watching over all their flocks, keeping them safe from wild animals and thieves. Sometime during the night, "an angel of the Lord appeared to them, and the glory of the Lord shone

around them, and they were terrified" (Luke 2:9).
Just like Mary and Joseph had no idea of the great
and awesome things God had in store for their
lives, so too were the shepherds unaware of the
beautiful and mighty life change they were about
to experience.

Even though they were terrified, the angel tried
to calm the shepherds and told them not to be
afraid. The angel went on to explain that a Savior
had been born in Bethlehem and then instructed
the men to go and find baby Jesus in the manger.

The shepherds hurried and found Mary,
Joseph, and the baby, just as they were told! The
shepherds quickly spread the good news about
what they had witnessed. Mary, on the other hand,
"treasured up all these things and pondered them
in her heart" (Luke 2:19). That means Mary held
on to these moments and reflected on them in quiet
meditation. This holy night, and everything it

stood for, would remain in Mary's heart forever.

Shortly after His birth, Mary and Joseph gave their new baby the name Jesus, just as the angel had told them. Jesus. Messiah. Savior of the

World. Redeemer. How proud Mary must have been as she watched strangers' lives change and their hearts open when they came into contact with her son.

Not long after the miraculous and beautiful birth of Jesus, Joseph and Mary took Him to the temple in Jerusalem to present Him to the Lord. There, the Bible says, they met a man named

Simeon who was very nice. Simeon saw baby Jesus and held Him in his arms. He called out to God, saying that his eyes had seen the Savior!

Mary and Joseph marveled at what was said about Jesus (Luke 2:33). A prophet named Anna, who was very old, stayed in the temple worshipping God day and night. She too came up to Mary and Joseph, gave thanks, and spoke highly of Jesus and talked about how He would be the One who would redeem people.

After all the jobs in Jerusalem were complete, Mary and Joseph returned to Nazareth. Jesus "grew and became strong; he was filled with wisdom, and the grace of God was on him" (Luke 2:40).

Wise Men Visit

The birth of Jesus was very special. Soon people everywhere were hearing the news of His arrival. While Mary was raising her newborn son, wise men (magi) from the East came to Jerusalem and asked where they could find the "king of the Jews" (Matthew 2:2). When they arrived, the men approached a king named Herod, who wasn't a good man. The king told them to report back after they found Jesus. He said it was because he also wanted to go and worship Jesus; but truthfully, Herod had different plans. He didn't want Jesus taking over his role as king, so he made an evil plan to end Jesus' life.

The magi left Herod and went on their way. Soon they found the house they were looking for.

They found Mary and Jesus at home. Even though we aren't given specifics in the Bible, we can imagine the look on Mary's face when these strangers appeared at her door saying that they had followed a star in the night sky to find them.

The magi explained the reason for their visit. And like the shepherds before them, the men bowed down and worshipped Jesus. Their worship of Jesus gives more proof that He was the King of kings they had been looking for. Mary watched in awe as the men presented Jesus with gifts of gold, frankincense, and myrrh (Matthew 2:11). These gifts would help Mary and Joseph avoid staying in poverty. God had blessed the young couple and their young son.

Sometime during this visit, the wise men were warned in a dream not to return to King Herod. They said goodbye to Mary, Joseph, and Jesus and took a different route back to their homes.

After the men left, an angel came to Joseph in a dream and told him to take Jesus and Mary and escape to Egypt. The angel told Joseph about King Herod's wicked plans to hurt Jesus. So, under cover of night, Joseph took Mary and Jesus and left

Bethlehem. They headed for the faraway land of Egypt where they stayed until Herod died.

Instead of returning to Bethlehem, Mary and Joseph traveled to Nazareth. They made this decision because Herod's son Archelaus reigned over Bethlehem, and they didn't want to risk any harm coming to Jesus.

All the traveling and all the escapes. Visits from angels, shepherds, and wise men. Mary

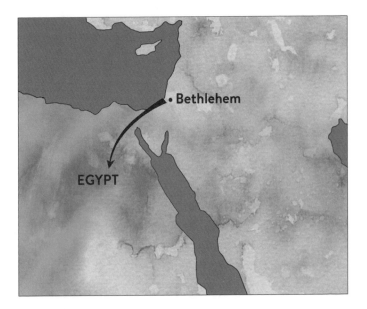

couldn't have imagined a more bizarre story, but she remained faithful to God through it all. She knew that God could have changed the way things happened to her and her family. Jesus could have come into the world in a totally different, much more triumphant, way. Definitely not in an animal pen on a cold, dark night with nothing but strips of cloth to keep Him warm. That's not how the King of kings should enter the scene, right?

But that's exactly how God wanted it to be. And Mary's heart embraced the plans and desires of her

CLUES

The Bible doesn't tell us how long Mary, Joseph, and Jesus stayed in Egypt. Some say anywhere between months and years. But whatever the length of time, it's important to focus on Mary's obedience to God's will. God could have made a way for Herod to be taken off the throne, but instead God chose to have Mary and Joseph take Jesus far away from their home.

heavenly Father. She didn't
argue or complain. Mary just trusted God's will
and humbled herself to accept the strange circum-
stances that surrounded the birth of Jesus.

Jesus at the Temple

When time came for the Passover festival, Mary and Joseph took Jesus to Jerusalem for this annual event. Passover was a time when the people celebrated and remembered how God freed their ancestors from slavery in Egypt. You might remember a man named Moses. He was the man who helped free the Israelites from under the pharaoh's rule. During that time, God sent ten plagues over Egypt. During the last plague, the Spirit of the Lord passed over the homes of the Israelites, keeping them from harm.

Mary and Joseph followed the rules and obeyed the laws. They were dedicated Jews living according to the law of Moses. In those days, a boy of twelve was considered to be completing his last year of preparation for religious life. Up to that point in a young man's life, the parents (especially the father) would teach the boy the commandments. At the end of the twelfth year, a formal ceremony took place in which the son would become a *bar mitzvah,* or "son of the commandment."

Jesus was around twelve years old at the time and was strong and filled with wisdom, and the grace of God was on Him (Luke 2:40). It seems as though Jesus had chosen this crucial time to show everyone that He had a unique relationship with God and an extraordinary understanding of God's law.

When the Passover festival was over, Mary and Joseph headed back home to Nazareth. When they left, Jesus stayed behind in Jerusalem. His parents were unaware that Jesus wasn't traveling with them. Remember, they were most likely traveling with a large group of family and friends and had assumed Jesus was in the crowd. Mary traveled for a full day before she began looking for Jesus among her relatives and friends.

After searching for a long time, Mary could not find her son, so both she and Joseph returned to

Jerusalem to look for Jesus. Surely they worried about where He was or what might have happened to Him.

After three whole days of searching, Mary found Jesus in the temple courts, "sitting among the

CLUES

Jesus traveling apart from His parents suggests that they trusted Him. He was trustworthy enough that Mary didn't worry. A good lesson here is to act respectfully to your parents and teachers. Let your actions show others that you care more about doing God's will than your own.

teachers, listening to them and asking them questions" (Luke 2:46). Mary stood there astonished, not only at the fact that she had found her son, but by the looks on the people's faces who were listening to Jesus speak. "Everyone who heard him was amazed at his understanding and his answers" (Luke 2:47).

Mary, however, was not all pleased with Jesus. She said, "Son, why have you treated us like this? Your father and I have been anxiously searching for you" (Luke 2:48).

Jesus had an answer ready for His mother. He asked her

CLUES

Mary and Joseph's three-day ordeal of searching and painfully regretting losing track of their son foreshadowed the pain that would come when Mary had to endure the crucifixion and burial of Jesus. After another three days of agony and grieving her son's death, a day of rejoicing would come when Mary realized that Jesus had conquered death!

why they were searching for Him. He said, "Didn't you know I had to be in my Father's house?" The Bible says that Mary and Joseph didn't understand what Jesus meant by His question. It's clear, however, that Jesus understood that His heavenly Father had sent Him on a mission to become the Savior of the world. Also, Jesus knew that His relationship to God was more important than any other relationship.

Jesus was basically telling His parents that He had come into this world to do His Father's business. After the meeting back at the temple, Jesus did follow Mary and Joseph home to Nazareth and "was obedient to them" (Luke 2:51). The next verse in Luke's account is an important one as we learn about Mary's personality and what made her special. It says that she "treasured all these things in her heart" (2:51). What things? The words Jesus was saying. Even though she might not have understood everything Jesus was doing, Mary chose to keep all of it in her heart, believing that as time went on things would be made clear to her.

Mary watched her son grow wiser and stronger. She watched as He gained favor with both God and man.

A Special Wedding

In a remote village away from the hustle of Jerusalem, a couple was getting married in a place called Cana in Galilee. Mary, Jesus, and His disciples were at the wedding celebration. The Bible doesn't mention Joseph, because he had most likely passed away by this time in Mary's life. The wedding was a big celebration, and everyone was having a good time.

At some point, after the people had been eating and drinking, the Bible says that Mary went up to Jesus and told Him that the hosts of the party had run out of wine. Jesus answered, "Woman, why do you involve me? My hour has not yet come" (John 2:4). He was explaining to Mary that there is an appointed time for everything

in God's plan. Jesus was saying that He answers

only to God. And the "hour" referred to the hour

when Jesus would die for the sins of the world.

Jesus confirmed that He would be obedient to God

above all others. He was setting the example that even though she was His mother, Mary would not be treated differently than any of God's other children.

Jesus did perform a miracle to help Mary and the wedding guests. He probably also performed it to give the guests a picture of His upcoming sacrifice on the cross. And even though Jesus rebuked Mary (told her seriously that He had come to do God's will), she was confident in her relationship and worth in Jesus. She went on to tell the servants, "Do whatever he tells you" (John 2:5).

Mary stood by and watched Jesus tell the servants to fill six stone jars (each held twenty to

thirty gallons). The attendants obeyed and filled the ceremonial jars to the brim. These were not jars used for drinking. These jars would be used for the ritual washing for purification. This means the people would have religious ceremonies and use the jars of water to represent the washing away of bad choices.

Next, Jesus told them to draw out some water and take it to the man who was in charge of the banquet.

CLUES

Mary set an example for all of us as she showed us boldness in approaching Jesus as the answer to and provider for all our problems. And even though this was the first public miracle that Jesus performed, Mary knew that her son was capable of great things. Mary set a good example for us not only to ask God for help for ourselves, but also to ask Him to help others in need. We bring God glory when we lift others up in prayer. She knew there were other ways to solve the problem, but going to Jesus is always the best answer.

When the master tasted the water, he was amazed because it was actually wine. Another interesting note is that the bridegroom was in charge

of the wine and would have been responsible for seeing that it did not run out before the party was over.

The Bible says that Jesus decided to perform the miracle to display His glory. Also, because of this miracle, the disciples believed in Him. Jesus showed the wedding guests—and us today—that He alone can provide what man cannot. Mary knew that all of this grace shown at the wedding in Cana had nothing to do with her.

After the wedding feast, Mary traveled with Jesus and His brothers and disciples to Capernaum where they stayed a few days. Surely their conversation along the way was about the miracle Jesus had performed at the wedding!

A Misunderstanding, the Cross, and Everything After

Time passed after the wedding feast. Jesus entered a house with His friends and planned to eat a meal there. As usual, a large crowd gathered inside. People had heard about Jesus and all of His love and healing power. They poured into the house to try and get Jesus to help them too. The gathering was so big that Jesus and His followers were not able to eat.

His family heard about this and came to get Jesus. They came to take Him away, thinking that He was out of His mind. They thought He might be tired because of all the work He had been doing.

The teachers of the law came down from Jerusalem and said that Jesus was possessed by the devil because He was driving out demons. They didn't believe Jesus was who He said He was, so these men were looking for a way to get rid of Jesus.

Jesus firmly corrected them, saying they

should not blaspheme (or make fun of) the Holy Spirit. He was trying to tell the people that He was doing God's work and that indeed He had not lost His mind.

When Mary arrived with Jesus' brothers, they stood outside of the house where Jesus was. They sent someone in to call Jesus out. The crowd inside told Jesus that Mary and His brothers were looking for Him. Jesus answered with a question: "Who are my mother and my brothers?" (Mark 3:33). Without waiting for an answer, Jesus told those gathered around Him that whoever does God's will is His family.

***

The next time Mary is mentioned by name in the Bible is when Jesus was being crucified. This was the darkest hour. Mary had to endure great pain and sadness as the soldiers made Jesus carry His cross all through the streets of Jerusalem and then out of the city to a place called Golgotha ("the place of the skull"). Mary watched as the soldiers nailed Jesus to the cross. She saw the sign that was placed over His head: This Is Jesus, the King of the Jews. The soldiers wrote the sign in Latin, Greek, and Aramaic to make sure everyone around could read the charge made against Jesus.

Mary, who had been storing the memories of Jesus in her heart, now understood how true that sign on her son's cross really was. The Bible tells us the chief priests complained. They wanted the sign to read that Jesus "claimed to be king of the Jews" (John 19:21). The sign remained, and the soldiers divided up the Lord's clothes.

Poor Mary had a place right at the foot of the cross. She was there with her sister and Mary Magdalene. Also, the disciple John was there. Jesus spoke to both of them from the cross. "Woman, here is your son," and to the disciple, "Here is your mother." (John 19:26–27). From that day, John took Mary into his home to live.

As the sadness continued, Mary watched as Jesus took His last breath. And after His body was taken down off the cross, another friend of Jesus',

a man named Joseph of Arimathea, came and took His body away to be buried in a new tomb nearby. The Bible doesn't tell us what Mary was doing at that point, but she was likely overcome with grief and emotion. However, she would have been fa-

miliar with her son's teachings and His words that spoke of rising from the grave after three days. Somewhere in Mary's heart, hope was waiting and looking forward to a day when all of her tears would be wiped away.

***

The last time Mary is mentioned by name in the Bible happens after Jesus rose from the grave. Jesus appeared to His apostles for a period of forty days, teaching them more truths about the kingdom of God. One day, Jesus gave them a command not to leave the city of Jerusalem until they received the gift of the Holy Spirit. Jesus told them that with the Holy Spirit, they would be His witnesses to the ends of the earth. Just after saying this, Jesus was taken up into heaven and a cloud hid Him from them.

The apostles stood staring at the sky when two men dressed in white clothing asked what they were looking at. The two men went on to explain that Jesus would return in the same way He went to heaven.

All of Jesus' friends, including Mary and His

brothers, gathered together, constantly praying to God. They were celebrating because Jesus was alive. They were also looking for direction. After all, they had just watched Jesus go up into heaven and were left to wonder about their future.

Now that we've investigated the story of Mary, mother of Jesus, it's time to study some lessons that we can learn from her life. We will look at ten "Power-Ups" that will help us connect scripture to our daily lives. Memory verses will go along with each Power-Up to help us plant God's truth in our hearts.

Power-Up #1:

LET YOUR LIFE GLORIFY GOD.

Mary prayed for her soul to make God magnified. You know when you look at something through a magnifying glass, it gets bigger. When people look at your life, do they see a bigger picture of who God is? This is what Mary wanted for her life. She was focused on letting her actions point people to God in big ways. When we read our Bibles and plant God's words deep in our hearts, we will live a life that brings Him glory.

It's one thing to read a few Bible stories and listen to sermons in church, but it's another thing to live out your beliefs. Mary was so familiar with the Old Testament that she was able to sing out her song of praise as she quoted scripture. Think about your schedule and come up with a plan to have a daily quiet time with God. This will help you know God more and understand how to live a life that makes much of Him. This is a good goal to make as we work on powering up our daily walks with Jesus.

Think of ways you can make more of God. Ask Him for strength and opportunities to turn people toward His mercy and grace. Let God use you like He used Mary, by sacrificing your time and resources to share the good news of Jesus. Do things that let other people know they are loved by God. Memorize scripture so you can plant the Word of God in your heart so you will be able to recite verses of praise and instruction as you follow God's will for your life.

MEMORY VERSE: "My soul glorifies the Lord." Luke 1:46

Power-Up #2:

REJOICE THAT GOD IS YOUR SAVIOR.

The next part of Mary's song gives us another goal to strive for in living life for God. She knew that her spirit was the fullest when it was praising her Savior. When we find our greatest joy in Jesus, we will be completely satisfied. The enemy will try to tempt God's children into finding their happiness in other people and material possessions. You may find yourself wishing you had more than what you have. You may find yourself complaining because things didn't go exactly the way you wanted them to.

But God wants us to rely on Him in all situations. Whether your day is going great or your heart is filled with sadness, God wants you to know how much you mean to Him. Try to praise Him daily and let Him carry you in His mighty arms. This helps take your eyes off of yourself and put them on God. Having a grateful heart keeps your priorities straight. You will get to a place where praising God becomes a habit. Instead of complaining about what didn't go right, you will find yourself contemplating all the wonderful things God is and thanking Him for loving you.

Be happy with where God has you. Thank Him for providing for all your needs. Trust that He has the best plans for you. Trust that He wants everything you want and more. Spend your time finding ways to praise Him. Rejoice that God has saved you from the chains of sin. You will make mistakes, but the difference is that you're forgiven. Like Mary, we need to let our lives announce the joy that we find only in Jesus.

MEMORY VERSE: "My spirit rejoices in God my Savior." Luke 1:47

Power-Up #3:
GOD KNOWS YOU.

What a strong, encouraging truth to take with you in your days, to know that God knows your name! The Creator of the universe knows you and thinks about you. He considers all the wonderful plans He has for your life and leads you daily to all the things He has in store for you. Mary said that God was *mindful* of her (Luke 1:48). This means that God cared about every detail of her life, and since God doesn't change, we can be confident that He does the same for us today.

You are the only *you* God made! There never has been another *you*, and there never will be another. As you think about this powerful truth, let it move your heart as you begin to ponder how much kingdom work you can accomplish for God's glory. What special talents has God given you? What are you really good at doing? How can you take those gifts and use them to bless others and point people to Jesus as their Savior? God thinks about you all day long. He celebrates your accomplishments, and He understands your sadness. You are not alone. God is always thinking about you.

God made you special. He thought long and hard about how to make you unique. He made no mistakes when He created you. Don't forget that truth! He knows all of you, and the Bible promises that He has great plans for your life. You aren't like one of those wind-up toys, as if God sets you in motion and then leaves you on your own to go on random paths. You are an original masterpiece whom God carries through all of the hours and days He has planned for you. Celebrate your wonderful Creator today. He really does care!

MEMORY VERSE: "He has been mindful of the humble state of his servant." Luke 1:48

Power-Up #4:

GOD BLESSES YOU.

When Mary prayed, she said that generations of
people would call her blessed. She wasn't being
prideful. She was simply confident in her identity
in Jesus. She knew her worth wasn't found in
worldly things. As a believer, your life, identity,
and worth are all wrapped up in Jesus. Our lesson
here to power up our daily living is to remember
that we are leaving a legacy of mercy and grace.
People are always watching us. They may never
tell us, but they are looking at how we treat each
other and how we talk. They are seeing if our
words match our actions.

We should live a life that makes people want
to praise God's name forever. Our choices should
reflect the light of Jesus in a dark world. Think
about all the ways God has blessed you. Let this
fill your heart with gladness as you go through
your day. Be confident that God loves you and is

always at work in your life. Be certain that He calls you to step out in faith to do big things. This begins the work of creating a legacy where future family members will share stories about your wonderful kingdom work!

God knows what we need before we even ask Him for anything. He gives us what we need and so much more. When you realize just how much He blesses you, things start to look different. You begin to nurture a heart of greater thankfulness and compassion. Being aware of your blessings helps you to share those blessings with others. Maybe you could start a prayer journal and list all the ways God is blessing you. That could drive your prayers and praises throughout the year. It will also help you see how God is working and moving in your life.

MEMORY VERSE: "From now on all generations will call me blessed." Luke 1:48

Power-Up #5:

GOD DOES GREAT THINGS FOR YOU.

God is always doing great things for us. Since God doesn't change, we need to always remember that He wants what's best for us. He doesn't walk away or stop listening. Live each day knowing that God is your Mighty One. He is the source of all your hope. God will never walk away from you or change the way He feels about your heart. Pray and wait. Know that God doesn't make mistakes. God is working in your life in mighty ways to bless you.

Live by the strength that comes from the same One who put the stars in the sky and carved out the massive oceans and filled them with water. God knows what you need because He made you! Whatever you're facing, God will do great things for you because He loves you more than anything. Trust this even when the day is long and you feel tired. Trust that God is doing great things for you even when happiness seems just out of reach.

Wrap your mind around the fact that God is *for* you. He wants to see you thrive and be a powerful witness to His kingdom. He wants you to know that you aren't just another person lost in the crowd. God is cheering you on to lead the crowd for Jesus! It's exciting to think about all the possibilities you have in front of you. Your life will continue to shine by God's radiant light and continually remind the world that His name is forever holy.

MEMORY VERSE: "The Mighty One has done great things for me—holy is his name." Luke 1:49

Power-Up #6:

GOD GIVES YOU HIS MERCY.

God knows what you're going through. He sees
the path you're on and walks beside you. Just like
He did for Mary, God will also show you mercy all
the time. When Mary was nervous about the news
of being pregnant, God showed mercy and sent
an angel to help soothe her. When Mary needed
reassurance, God brought her to Elizabeth and let
them connect with the Holy Spirit. When Jesus
was older and they were at the wedding feast,
Mary found comfort in the power of her son's abil-
ity to provide.

God is there for you today. He is ready to give you
mercy and lift you up because He cares about you so
much. Know that His mercy is active. It picks you
up from the pit of your mistakes and bad choices
and sets you down on the solid ground of God's
truth. His mercy holds your hand and reassures
you that everything will be okay. He thinks you're

awesome, and His mercy reminds you of that truth. God wants you to know that He listens to you and thinks about you. Be encouraged by how much you mean to Him, and live today for His kingdom!

God's mercy showers you with second chances. His mercy means that when you mess up or make a bad choice, God is not going to walk away from you. Ever. From the very beginning of the Bible, God didn't leave Adam and Eve alone in the garden. He went after them and provided a sacrifice and clothing. God solved their sin problem. God's mercy solves your problems too. You have to work hard and honor Him in everything you do, but when things don't go the way you hoped, God's mercy reminds you that He is in control and He cares for you.

MEMORY VERSE: "His mercy extends to those who fear him." Luke 1:50

Power-Up #7:

GOD IS MIGHTY AND CARRIES YOUR BURDENS.

The One who made you and loves you also is strong enough to carry you. Whatever you're going through, God is bigger! Even though we can't imagine how sad Mary must have been to see Jesus carry His cross to Calvary, it must have been amazing to see her face when she realized that Jesus defeated the grave and rose again! Mary understood pain and loss. She saw how the cross weighed heavy on her son's back. She experienced loss when, as a youth, Jesus had stayed behind in the temple after she and Joseph had left for home.

No power on earth is stronger than God. Put your trust in Him, and He will never let you down. Just as Mary relied on God to get her through the hard times, we need to do the same. God loves you and is there to carry you through it all. No matter how alone you might feel, God is always with you.

He holds you and never lets go. This should re-assure you that nothing gets to you before it goes through God. He is your shield and protector. Give Him your hardships. Give Him your sadness. God is there to give you rest.

God is the Rock on which your life is built. No storm or trial is bigger than God. Nothing in this world is strong enough to pull you down and away from Him. He protects you with His mighty arms. He wipes away tears and encourages you because He is full of love and compassion. Remember that He is for you in all things, and His love is forever.

MEMORY VERSE: "He has performed mighty deeds with his arm." Luke 1:51

Power-Up #8:

GOD LIFTS UP THE HUMBLE.

Mary obeyed God and lived a humble life. She knew that God had a plan for her, and she was satisfied with that plan. Mary wanted God to be in charge of her life. It's easy to get wrapped up in wanting more than you have or even wishing you had all the things your friends have. But God has a plan for you, and He will give you everything you need to be successful. He doesn't want you distracted by running after stuff.

Being humble means relying on God all the time, not just when we need something. Let Him show you the paths He wants you to take, and be content with them. Being humble means accepting that God's plans may not be what we want but still being okay because we know that God wants what's best for His children. Being humble often means putting others' needs before your own. It's not easy, but that is the example Jesus set for us, and He guarantees to lift up and help those who live out of humility rather than selfish pride.

At times you will feel like being selfish. This is when you have an opportunity to pray and ask God for help in being humble to put other people first. Putting other people's needs before your own helps you to become more like Jesus!

MEMORY VERSE: "[He] has lifted up the humble." Luke 1:52

Power-Up #9:

GOD MEETS ALL YOUR NEEDS.

Mary knew God was her provider. She understood that He was the One who gave her everything she needed. She knew that He had chosen her to give birth to baby Jesus and gave her all the many blessings that came with being His mother. Mary understood that everything she had came from God and not from her hard work. God was in control of her life, and He provided for her and her family.

God does the same thing for us. He meets us where we are, no matter what situation we find ourselves in, and takes care of our needs. Even if we're having a bad day and God seems far away, the truth will always be that He is with us. Be confident that you are very special to Him. The Bible is full of examples of how much God provides. When people were hungry, God gave them bread from heaven. When they were outnumbered in battle, God gave them protection. And when people needed a Savior, God gave them Jesus! He knows what we need! Talk to God. Tell Him what you need. He knows and loves you. Be amazed at how He will bless your life!

This doesn't mean that God is a vending machine who will give you whatever you ask for. It means that God knows the best things for you. He decides. Knowing this will free you from worrying about things. Give everything to God and be free to follow Him.

MEMORY VERSE: "He has filled the hungry with good things." Luke 1:53

Power-Up #10:

GOD IS HELPFUL.

Remember how Mary lived a humble life, connected to Jesus all the time? She knew that He was the source of her hope and provider for all that mattered. Mary relied on Jesus to be her helper, and that's a great way for us to live today. Like Mary, we need to get in the habit of turning to Jesus.

From that humble start in the stable, holding baby Jesus began the unbreakable bond of mother and child. In that moment as Mary held Jesus, she knew that her baby would grow and become so much more than her son. Jesus would become her source for living.

In the beginning of His ministry, at the wedding feast, Mary didn't hesitate to ask Jesus to turn the water into wine. Jesus took care of His mother then, and because of His great love for her, He took care of her at the end of His earthly life. From the cross, Jesus made sure His friend John would take care of Mary.

Turning to Jesus and relying on Him will help us become the people we were made to be, and in turn, God will be glorified.

MEMORY VERSE: "He has helped his servant." Luke 1:54

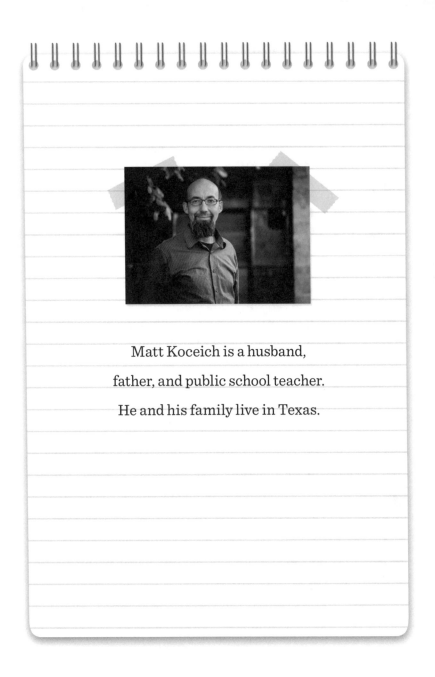

Matt Koceich is a husband,
father, and public school teacher.
He and his family live in Texas.

Collect Them All!

Kingdom Files: Who Is Jesus?

This biblically accurate biography explores the life of Jesus while drawing readers into a fascinating time and place as they learn about the One who gave sight to the blind, made the lame to walk, raised people from the dead, and who died so that we might live.

Paperback / 978-1-68322-626-0 / $4.99

Kingdom Files: Who Was Daniel?

This biblically accurate biography explores the life of Daniel while drawing readers into a fascinating time and place as they learn about the faithful man of God who interpreted dreams for the king and ultimately survived a den of hungry lions.

Paperback / 978-1-68322-627-7 / $4.99

Kingdom Files: Who Was David?

This biblically accurate biography explores the life of David while drawing readers into a fascinating time and place as they learn about the shepherd boy turned king who played a harp and slayed a giant with a stone and a sling.

Paperback / 978-1-68322-628-4 / $4.99

Kingdom Files: Who Was Jonah?

This biblically accurate biography explores the life of Jonah while drawing readers into a fascinating time and place as they learn about the reluctant prophet who said "no" to God, was tossed overboard during a storm, and swallowed by a giant fish.

Paperback / 978-1-68322-630-7 / $4.99

Kingdom Files: Who Was Esther?

This biblically accurate biography explores the life of Esther while drawing readers into a fascinating time and place as they learn about the beautiful Queen of Persia who hid her Jewish heritage from the king and ultimately risked her life to save her people.

Paperback / 978-1-68322-629-1 / $4.99

Excited for More?

Here's a sneak peek of
Kingdom Files: Who Was David?

1

Early Life

To begin our investigation into the life of David, it helps to understand a few background notes first. David's story is found in the Old Testament books of 1 Samuel, 2 Samuel, 1 Kings, and 1 Chronicles. When David was young, a king named Saul had ruled over the land of Israel for forty-two years. He became selfish, so God decided to call a new young man to take the throne.

God sent his prophet, Samuel, to David's house. So Samuel went to Bethlehem where he found a man named Jesse, who was David's father. David was the youngest of eight sons. He worked as a shepherd tending his father's

flock. Jesse introduced his sons to Samuel, but the prophet asked if there were any others. That's when Jesse called for David, and immediately Samuel knew this was who he was supposed to anoint as king. The Bible says that at this point, the Spirit of God came on David with power (1 Samuel 16:13).

Meanwhile, King Saul was being attacked by an evil spirit. He asked his servants to bring someone who could play music to help calm his

nerves. The servants knew about David, and so Jesse sent his son David to Saul with a donkey loaded with bread and wine and a young goat as gifts for the king. Saul was so pleased with David and his music playing that he had David stay with him to be in his service.

At the same time, there was an army called the Philistines who were close by, trying to attack the Israelites. King Saul gathered the

Israelites to fight and defend their towns (1 Samuel 17:2–3). When they went out to engage in battle, Saul and his men were confronted by a horrifying sight. There was one Philistine in particular named Goliath. The Bible says that Goliath was over nine feet tall and wore a bronze hel-met and armor that

CLUES

Even the giant's spear had a fifteen-pound iron point!

weighed 125 pounds!

The giant began taunting the king and his army. Goliath yelled out a challenge. He asked for a man who would be willing to fight him. He said that if he won, the Israelites would become slaves to the Philistines; and if one of Saul's men won, the Philistines would become servants to the Israelites. King Saul was terrified! (1 Samuel 17:11).

This exchange went on for forty days. Morning and night, Goliath approached the Israelites, asking for a man who would be willing to fight. No one dared fight the superhuman giant.

Meanwhile, David was in charge of taking food to his older brothers. They were a part of the Israelite army and within clear view of the giant. David ran out to the battle lines to check on his brothers and make sure they were okay. As soon as David saw Goliath, he wanted to know who

he was. David was upset because of the way the giant didn't respect God (1 Samuel 17:26).

David's oldest brother was angry at David because he thought David was only there to watch a good fight. Saul heard about David's courage and sent for him. In the king's chambers, David told Saul not to lose heart because of Goliath's threats. And then David offered to go and fight the giant!

Saul wasn't convinced. He thought David was too young and unable to win a battle with the giant. Saul added that Goliath had been a warrior for a very long time. But David was ready with a reply. He told Saul about his job tending sheep.

King Saul finally agreed with David and let him go and fight the giant. He began by putting his personal armor on David. But David couldn't move around in the heavy armor. David armed himself with only his staff and his sling, and he chose five stones from a nearby stream and put them in a pouch. Then he went out to meet Goliath.

The superhuman laughed. "Am I a dog, that you come at me with sticks? . . . Come here. . . and I'll give your flesh to the birds and the wild animals!" (1 Samuel 17:43–44). David knew that God was on his side and responded to the giant not with fear but with courage. "You come against me with sword and spear and javelin, but I come against you in the name of the LORD Almighty"

(1 Samuel 17:45). David said that he was confident that God would deliver the giant into his hands. And then he added that after he won the battle, the

whole world would know that God was in charge.

David also said that the battle belonged to God and that God would give not only Goliath but all the Philistines into the Israelites' hands. At that, the giant moved quickly to attack David. David didn't hesitate. He ran toward the giant. As he ran, David took a stone and slung it at Goliath. The stone hit the giant on the forehead, causing him to fall dead "facedown on the ground" (1 Samuel 17:49). At the sight of this unbelievable event, the Philistines took off running. David kept Goliath's weapons. King Saul was very impressed that David had taken care of the wicked giant and a very massive problem!